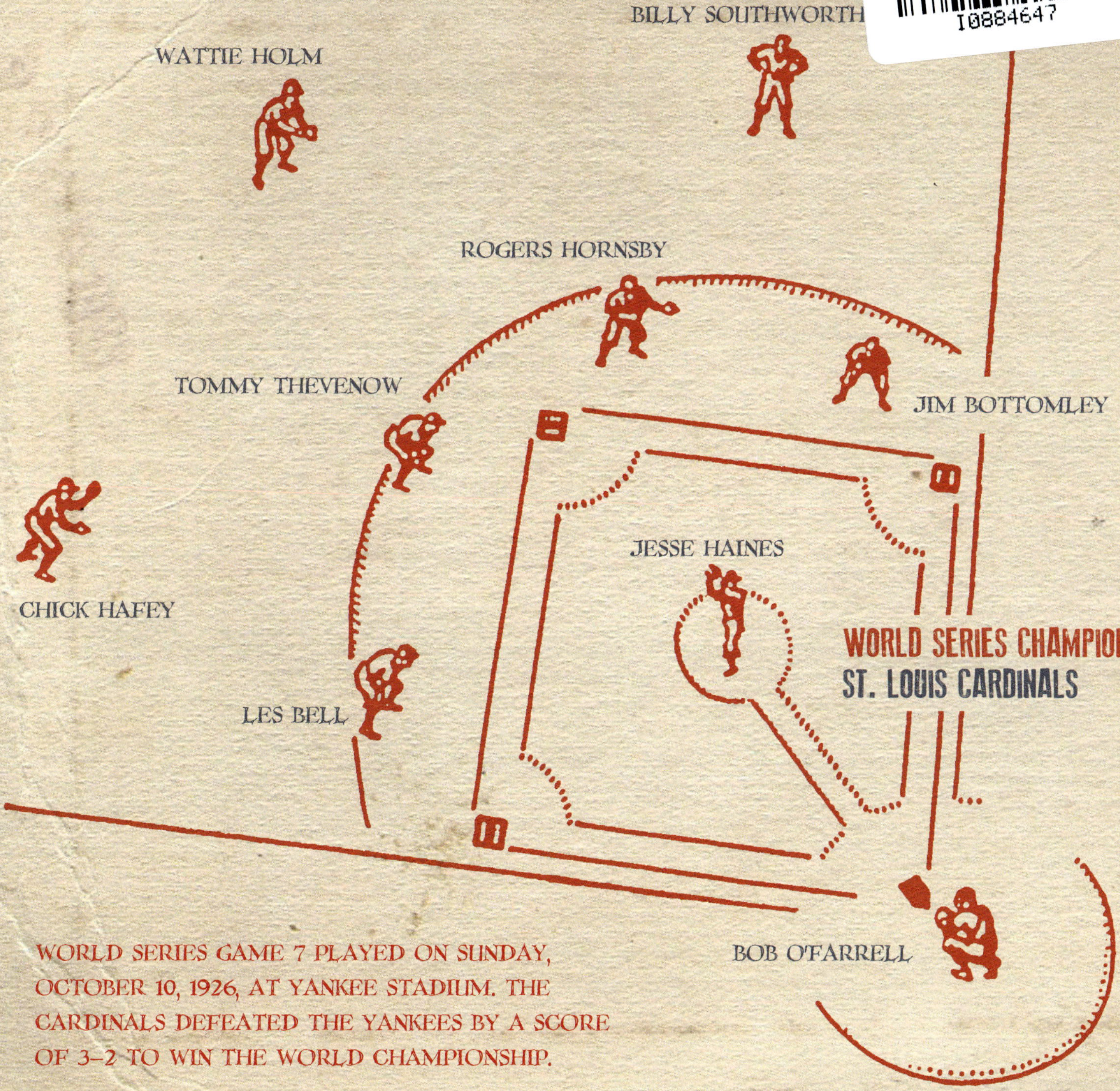

WORLD SERIES CHAMPIONS
ST. LOUIS CARDINALS

WORLD SERIES GAME 7 PLAYED ON SUNDAY, OCTOBER 10, 1926, AT YANKEE STADIUM. THE CARDINALS DEFEATED THE YANKEES BY A SCORE OF 3–2 TO WIN THE WORLD CHAMPIONSHIP.

I0884647

Cardinals
23

WORLD SERIES CHAMPIONS

ST. LOUIS CARDINALS

SARA GILBERT

CREATIVE PAPERBACKS

Published by Creative Paperbacks
P.O. Box 227, Mankato, Minnesota 56002
Creative Paperbacks is an imprint of The Creative Company
www.thecreativecompany.us

Design and production by Blue Design (www.bluedes.com)
Art direction by Rita Marshall
Printed in the United States of America

Photographs by Corbis (Bettmann), Getty Images (Bernstein Associates, Bruce Bennett Studios, Dan Donovan/MLB Photos, Elsa, Ron T. Ennis/Fort Worth Star-Telegram/MCT, FPG, Focus on Sport, Hulton Archive, Rob Leiter/MLB Photos, G. Newman Lowrance, Brad Mangin/MLB Photos, MLB Photos, National Baseball Hall of Fame Library/MLB Photos, New York Times Company, Photo File, Louis Requena/MLB Photos, Josh Umphrey, Tim Umphrey, Ron Vesely/MLB Photos, Grey Villet/Time & Life Pictures, Dilip Vishwanat, Jeremy Woodhouse)

Copyright © 2013 Creative Paperbacks
International copyright reserved in all countries. No part of this book may be reproduced in any form without written permission from the publisher.

Library of Congress Cataloging-in-Publication Data
Gilbert, Sara.
St. Louis Cardinals / Sara Gilbert.
p. cm. — (World series champions)
Includes bibliographical references and index.
Summary: A simple introduction to the St. Louis Cardinals major league baseball team, including its start in 1882, its World Series triumphs, and its stars throughout the years.
ISBN 978-1-60818-271-8 (hardcover)
ISBN 978-0-89812-822-2 (pbk)
1. St. Louis Cardinals (Baseball team)—History—Juvenile literature.
I. Title.
GV875.S74G44 2013
796.357'640977866—dc23 2012004265

First edition
9 8 7 6 5 4 3 2 1

Cover: Pitcher Chris Carpenter
Page 2: Third baseman David Freese
Page 3: Pitcher Dizzy Dean
Right: A Cardinals game in 1950

32

RF
ENOS SLAUGHTER

1B
ORLANDO CEPEDA

3B
KEN BOYER

P
GROVER CLEVELAND ALEXANDER

M
WHITEY HERZOG

P
CY YOUNG

TABLE OF CONTENTS

ST. LOUIS AND BUSCH STADIUM 9

RIVALS AND COLORS 10

CARDINALS HISTORY 12

CARDINALS STARS 19

HOW THE CARDINALS GOT THEIR NAME 22

ABOUT THE CARDINALS 23

GLOSSARY 24

INDEX 24

ST. LOUIS AND BUSCH STADIUM

St. Louis is a big city in Missouri. It was **FOUNDED** in 1763 by explorers from France. St. Louis has a ballpark called Busch Stadium. That is the home field for a baseball team called the Cardinals.

RIVALS AND COLORS

The Cardinals play major league baseball. All the major-league teams hope to win the World Series and become world champions. The Cardinals wear red, white, and blue uniforms. Their main **RIVALS** are the Chicago Cubs.

LEFT FIELDER MATT HOLLIDAY

PITCHER BOB GIBSON

CARDINALS HISTORY

The Cardinals played their first season in 1882. They were known as the St. Louis Brown Stockings at first, and later as just the Browns. They became the Cardinals in 1900. For many years, they were stuck near the bottom of the **STANDINGS**.

1934 CARDINALS

C
TED SIMMONS

P
CHRIS CARPENTER

2B
SKIP SCHUMAKER

3B
SCOTT ROLEN

CF
WILLIE McGEE

1B
MARK McGWIRE

Star second baseman Rogers Hornsby joined St. Louis in 1915. The Cardinals started winning more games with Hornsby. In 1926, they won the World Series.

The Cardinals kept winning after that. They won the World Series in 1931 and 1934. From 1942 to 1946, sweet-swinging

STAN MUSIAL

outfielder Stan Musial led the Cardinals to the World Series four times. St. Louis won three of them.

With speedy left fielder Lou Brock on the team, the Cardinals were world champions in 1964 and 1967. Shortstop Ozzie Smith led St. Louis to another World Series win in 1982. In 2006, their first year in Busch Stadium, the Cardinals won their 10th championship. They were champs again in 2011!

LOU BROCK

OZZIE SMITH

CARDINALS STARS

Second baseman Frankie Frisch played for the Cardinals from 1927 to 1937. He and pitcher Dizzy Dean were part of a team nicknamed the "Gashouse Gang." They had fun winning lots of games together.

St. Louis missed the **PLAYOFFS** for eight straight years before Tony La Russa was hired as the Cardinals' manager in 1996. La Russa and fast center fielder Jim Edmonds helped the Cardinals get to the playoffs almost every season.

In 2001, first baseman Albert Pujols joined the Cardinals. He hit the ball so well that he won three Most Valuable Player awards. St. Louis fans hoped their favorite team would win more awards and championships soon!

JIM EDMONDS

ALBERT PUJOLS

HOW THE CARDINALS GOT THEIR NAME

In 1889, the owners of the St. Louis Browns changed their players' socks from brown to bright red. A sportswriter called the team the Cardinals because the new socks reminded him of the cheery, red songbirds. The name stuck!

PITCHER RYAN FRANKLIN

ABOUT THE CARDINALS

First season: 1882

League/division: National League, Central Division

World Series championships:

1926	*4 games to 3 versus New York Yankees*
1931	*4 games to 3 versus Philadelphia Athletics*
1934	*4 games to 3 versus Detroit Tigers*
1942	*4 games to 1 versus New York Yankees*
1944	*4 games to 2 versus St. Louis Browns*
1946	*4 games to 3 versus Boston Red Sox*
1964	*4 games to 3 versus New York Yankees*
1967	*4 games to 3 versus Boston Red Sox*
1982	*4 games to 3 versus Milwaukee Brewers*
2006	*4 games to 1 versus Detroit Tigers*
2011	*4 games to 3 versus Texas Rangers*

Cardinals Web site for kids:

http://mlb.mlb.com/mlb/kids/index.jsp?c_id=stl

Club MLB:

http://web.clubmlb.com/index.html

GLOSSARY

FOUNDED — started planning and building something, like a city

PLAYOFFS — all the games (including the World Series) after the regular season that are played to decide who the champion will be

RIVALS — teams that play extra hard against each other

STANDINGS — the rankings of sports teams from best to worst; they show how many wins and losses a team has

INDEX

Brock, Lou 17
Busch Stadium. 9, 17
Dean, Dizzy 19
Edmonds, Jim 20
Frisch, Frankie 19
"Gashouse Gang" 19
Hornsby, Rogers 15
La Russa, Tony 19
Most Valuable Player award . . 20
Musial, Stan 17
playoffs 19, 20
Pujols, Albert. 20
rivals 10
Smith, Ozzie 17
team colors 10
team name 12, 22
World Series. . . . 10, 15, 17, 23